In the Aftermath of the Tsunami

Photos From the Japan Tsunami

By S. Floyd Mori

In the Aftermath of the Tsunami

Photos From the Japan Tsunami

Copyright 2016

Photos by S. Floyd Mori

About the Author

S. Floyd Mori is an American of Japanese heritage. He was born and raised in Utah. After graduating from high school, he joined the United States Army Reserves. He started college at the University of Southern California and served a two-year mission for the Church of Jesus Christ of Latter-day Saints in Hawaii. He received a Bachelors and a Masters Degree from Brigham Young University with emphasis on Economics, Asian Studies, and Political Science.

After completing college, he taught Economics at Chabot College in Hayward, California, for ten years and served in the California State Assembly for six years. He was Mayor and City Councilman of the City of Pleasanton, California. He has been a Businessman and an International Business Consultant.

He is currently President/CEO of the Asian Pacific American Institute for Congressional Studies (APAICS) in Washington, D.C. APAICS is a national non-partisan, non-profit organization dedicated to promoting Asian Pacific American participation and representation at all levels of the political process from community service to elective office. The major programs of APAICS focus on developing leadership, building public policy knowledge, and filling the political pipeline for Asian Pacific Americans to pursue public office at the local, state, and federal levels.

He has been the National Executive Director/CEO of the Japanese American Citizens League (JACL), the oldest and largest Asian American civil and human rights organization in the United States. He was also President and Vice President on the National Board of the JACL. A major focus of the JACL is civil rights.

He was working for the JACL on March 11, 2011, when the massive earthquake and tsunami struck Japan. He was involved with providing opportunities for JACL members and supporters to help the country of Japan in the aftermath of the tsunami.

He has spoken and written extensively about civil rights and the Japanese American experience of World War II when 120,000 persons of Japanese ethnicity were forcibly removed from their west coast homes and incarcerated in camps in remote and desolate areas of the country. Because he was living in Utah as a small child, he did not personally experience the incarceration. He has studied the issue and has written about that period of history and about subsequent happenings within the Asian American community. Some of his work has been published in a book entitled, *The Japanese American Story As Told Through a Collection of Speeches and Articles.* He has published other books and ebooks including, *Bullying Is Not Just a Kids' Problem: It's a Matter of Civil Rights* and *Cherry Blossoms at the Tidal Basin: Washington, D.C. Photos.*

Floyd Mori may be contacted via email at: floydforest@gmail.com.

**Dedicated to the People of Japan
who suffered from the Tsunami**

CONTENTS

The massive destruction that hit Japan on March 11, 2011, was unprecedented. Japan is a country, which is arguably the best prepared in the world to handle natural disasters. They experience earthquakes on a fairly regular basis, but there is generally little damage from them. They have taken precautions and have warning systems to protect their people.

However, the magnitude of the huge natural disaster that afflicted Japan with the earthquake and resulting tsunami could not be predicted or avoided. Although the major devastation was in Northern Japan, it adversely affected the entire country and impacted the world as millions around the globe reached out in concern for the Japanese people.

The Japanese American Citizens League (JACL) is the oldest and largest Asian American civil and human rights organization in the United States. Their members and leadership were particularly moved to action as Japan is the country of ancestry for most of their members. There was immediate worry and fear for the safety of their friends and relatives in Japan. The JACL partnered with Direct Relief International to assist in relief efforts. They mobilized their chapters and members to offer assistance, as did many others from around the world.

The cherry blossoms that have such great meaning and significance for the people of Japan are a symbol of rebirth and new life. The people of Japan have received great challenges and hardships through the forces of nature. They will work hard and be resilient as the cherry blossoms in rebuilding and recovery.

The information contained herein is from personal knowledge, experience, and information readily available on the Internet.

Chapter One
The Tsunami Strikes, March 11, 2011

Friday, March 11, 2011, is a day that will be remembered forever by many people. At 2:46 p.m. on that day, a magnitude 9.0 earthquake struck offshore on the northeast coast of Japan, triggering a massive tsunami which caused extreme devastation and killed more than 18,000 people. The nuclear power plant in Fukushima was damaged as well, causing further problems.

Japanese people refer to the day as 3-11, a day etched in history, just as 9-11 is the reference to the day that terrorists struck the World Trade Center in New York City with commercial airplanes that caused many problems with that and other horrendous acts of terror to the United States of America on September 11, 2001.

A tsunami is caused by a large earthquake, volcanic eruption, or landslide under the ocean. It is a giant wave or series of waves that can have such force that it causes huge destruction of everything in its path. Tsunami waves move very fast when they are far out in the ocean. As a tsunami gets closer to the land, the speed of the wave slows down. However, the tsunami wave increases in height and has the potential to cause massive destruction.

Authorities in coastal regions may be on alert that a tsunami could have been triggered if a strong earthquake is noted. There is little notice, and they are unpredictable. This makes them extremely dangerous and something for which people are generally not able to prepare.

Although the Indian Ocean had the largest and the deadliest earthquake and tsunami during this century with 14 countries affected in 2004, the 3-11 event in Japan was unusually devastating for a country which is generally prepared for earthquakes. The northern region of Honshu, Japan's main island, had been forecast by scientists to have a smaller earthquake. They did not expect a disaster of such magnitude.

Tokyo residents were able to have a minute of warning before the strong earthquake started to shake the city. Japan has an earthquake early warning system. They also have stringent seismic building codes. These factors prevented many deaths from the earthquake by having the ability to stop high-speed trains and factory assembly lines. People in Japan were also able to receive alerts on their cell phones about the earthquake and impending tsunami. Still that day held much uncertainty and difficulty.

The first of the many tsunami waves hit Japan's coastline less than an hour after the earthquake struck. The tsunami waves reached up to 128 feet and traveled inland as much as six miles in some areas. The tsunami flooded approximately 217 square miles of land in northern Japan.

As of five years since the tsunami occurred, the confirmed death toll from the tsunami is over 18,000 including more than 2,500 still reported missing. Most of the people who died drowned.

Japan is normally well prepared for earthquakes and tsunamis even having built some protective seawalls at several locations. The massive tsunami wave destroyed those walls and even three story buildings. It was a disaster of huge proportions.

Chapter Two
Setting Up Ways to Help

While preparing to leave for the airport for a trip from Washington, D.C. to San Francisco early in the morning on March 11, 2011, I heard the horrible news of the huge earthquake and tsunami in Japan. I have been in Japan when earthquakes have occurred, and they generally caused little damage because the country is well prepared. However, this was much different. The tsunami caused massive destruction. All their preparations had not worked against this gigantic force of nature. It was immediate cause for concern as I and others in our organization of the Japanese American Citizens League (JACL) for which I was at the time the National Executive Director/CEO, have many friends and relatives living in Japan. In fact, the JACL has a chapter in Japan, and my two sons were living there as well.

I was immediately on the phone with numerous people who were concerned with being able to help the people of Japan through this disaster during an extremely difficult period of time. I was busy on the phone with the JACL leaders, the Japan Embassy personnel in Washington, D.C., and staff from the White House. We worked with the White House to prepare for a conference call with Japanese American and Japan Embassy leaders. The conference call took place that afternoon.

Calls with offers to help and donate money were coming in to the JACL offices. At first we suggested that people donate through another organization that was better equipped to handle the donations. It was an overwhelming outpouring of care and support for the people of Japan. Members and friends of the JACL and people from around the world wanted to help the victims of this disaster.

John Tagami, a close personal friend in Virginia, contacted me about the possibility of the JACL partnering with Direct Relief International, a premier disaster relief organization based in Santa Barbara, California. John is a friend of Thomas Tighe, the President of Direct Relief as they had worked together years before on Capitol Hill. After speaking with Thomas Tighe and doing some due diligence, we found that Direct Relief has decades of experience in emergency response and humanitarian assistance worldwide. They are a highly regarded organization.

Direct Relief International is California's largest medical relief organization and is active in all 50 states and 70 countries. They work with more than 1,000 health clinics across the United States to assist in emergencies on an ongoing basis. They provide people in need with free medications. Direct Relief was among the largest medical suppliers in Haiti in response to their 2010 earthquake.

With approval from the JACL National Board, a partnership between the JACL and Direct Relief was formed with the establishment of the Direct Relief/JACL Japan Relief and Recovery Fund. This fund would use all donations for the direct assistance of the victims of the disaster in Japan. There were so many inquiries from JACL members, coalition partners, associates, corporate sponsors, and friends who were anxious to help in a meaningful way. They wanted to join with the JACL in relief efforts.

The donations coming to the Japan Relief and Recovery Fund were intended to support the immediate health and human needs of victims by working with local NGO's (non-governmental agencies), which are basically non-profit organizations such as the JACL. The response was gratifying and impressive.

Since Direct Relief has been doing this type of relief work for a very long time, they have built relationships with businesses, groups, and individuals that immediately came forward with many donations and some very large contributions.

Members and corporate partners of the JACL also quickly began making financial donations to the Fund. With 100 chapters through the United States and a chapter in Japan, the JACL was positioned to maintain a close relationship to the work as it progressed on the ground in Japan. The basic grassroots nature of the JACL and the relationship with corporations and foundations gave the JACL a broad width and community thrust in working on the disaster relief.

One of our major corporate sponsors, UPS, phoned on the first day and offered a $50,000 grant to use as seen fit. A prominent foundation pledged a $50,000 anonymous donation. School children held fundraisers to help the people of Japan. The spirit of giving and wanting to lend a helping hand was overwhelming.

The Fund quickly received over $3.5 million, which includes some of Direct Relief's large donors who regularly give whenever any major disaster strikes anywhere in the world.

An arrangement by Direct Relief was made with a number of NBA players to join in the fundraising effort. Some of these professional basketball players paid $1,000 per point that they scored over a particular weekend to benefit the Fund. Others pledged a set amount. On that weekend, two NBA players, Lakers Pao Gasol and Bulls Derrick Rose scored 26 points and 23 points respectively, for which they donated $1,000 for each point. Magic Johnson said he would match Gasol's donation in an equal amount.

Direct Relief and the JACL participated in a press conference held in Sacramento to announce their partnership and relief efforts. Assembly Speaker John A. Perez and the Asian Pacific Islander Legislative Caucus joined in the press conference to offer support to Japan. Assembly member Warren Furutani encouraged Californians to lend a hand during Japan's time of need. Representatives of Cost Plus World Markets and Amgen were also on hand to announce their financial support.

The two organizations, Direct Relief and the JACL, started to work in earnest to secure donations and to determine the best ways that money could be used to benefit the people of Japan who were severely impacted by this monstrous disaster.

Thomas Tighe and I jointly issued the following statement from Direct Relief and the JACL: "This is a massive, complex emergency in Japan that we recognize is beyond the capacity of any one organization to address fully, so we believe this initial collaboration between our two longstanding, established organizations makes great sense, and we encourage other people, businesses, and organizations to join together to support people in Japan in this most difficult time."

In a later interview regarding the earthquake and tsunami, Brad Pitt acknowledged the efforts of Direct Relief and the JACL.

Chapter Three
Visiting the Destruction, March 29, 2011

Near the end of March about two weeks after the earthquake and tsunami hit, I was able to travel to Japan along with Brett Williams, who was Direct Relief's Director of International Programs and Emergency Response. We visited in Tokyo with partner organizations, JACL local leaders, and others, including my two sons who offered their assistance. Then we went to see the affected area firsthand. We did not travel at that time to the very hardest hit areas, but we witnessed large evidences of the severe devastation. We spoke with some victims and heard many stories of heartbreak and uprooted lives.

Our main purpose in traveling to Japan was to evaluate the effectiveness of our community NGO groups who were helping with the relief effort. We met with several and decided on at least four with whom we felt additional funding from our joint fund would be well deserved and useful. These groups rely on donations to keep up their good works. In stressful times, their resources are taxed to the limit.

The Japan Relief and Recovery Fund was able to distribute $400,000 to an NGO that has done heroic work in providing emergency goods such as fuel, tons of food, blankets, sleeping bags, and other supplies directly to the victims. They also planned to provide a medical unit with the grant that was given to them from our fund.

Passing out water

Demolished cars and trucks

Debris was all over

Houses were ruined

Inside an office

Streets were covered with rubble

Buildings were torn up and ruined

Boats were ruined

Buildings and homes were gutted

Large containers were moved

Cemetery destruction

Chapter Four
A Uniqlo Store

Uniqlo is a Japanese casual wear designer, manufacturer, and retailer. In addition to stores in Japan, Uniqlo operates in fourteen countries.

The company started as a men's clothing store called "Mens Shop OS" in 1949 in Yamaguchi, Japan. In 1984 they opened a unisex casual wear store in Hiroshima. It was called Unique Clothing Warehouse.

Later they planned to register under the brand of "Uniclo." However, a staff member in charge of the registration made a mistake and misread the "C" as a "Q" when the registration was done. That error caused the brand name to become "Uniqlo" which stands today.

By April 1994, there were over 100 Uniqlo stores operating throughout Japan. They have since gained prominence as they have spread around the world. It is now a brand with which most young people are familiar.

Former No. 1 player in the World Golf Ranking and currently No. 1 in the Fed Ex Standing, Adam Scott of Australia, can be seen at major golf tournaments shown on television wearing shirts that say "Uniqlo" on them. Other famous athletes wear the brand as well.

We visited a Uniqlo store on our trip to the devastated areas affected by the tsunami in Japan. This particular store was damaged extensively and was no longer operating. However, even with the windows broken so that people could freely enter the premises, the clothing was still intact in neat stacks just as had been the case before the tsunami struck. This store was damaged but not to the extent that all the contents were washed away and ruined. Many of the items were still in good shape although not clean and no longer ready to sell.

In other areas of the world and possibly particularly in the United States, looting immediately occurs when a disaster or social problem strikes. Perhaps the devastation was so great that the people had no need of such clothing. More likely, the people of Japan are basically an honest people who would not consider stealing and looting another's property for personal gain in times of disasters. People had lost everything and could probably have used some new clothing, but they did not steal goods from the damaged store shelves.

The victims of the Japan disaster stepped up to help others in need. Even though they were hurting themselves, they did what they could to alleviate the pain of those around them including their friends and family but also strangers in their midst.

We saw examples throughout the land of a people who were honest and true to their principles even during extremely difficult times.

It was a lesson learned and an example to the world.

Windows were broken out

Clothing remained intact as displayed

Shirts were still on the shelves

Clothing remained as displayed when the tsunami struck

Chapter Five
Help From Many Areas

It seemed that everyone wanted to help. The outpouring of donations and offers of assistance were overwhelming. The Japan Relief and Recovery Fund was growing, and we were able to assist NGO's with their work on the ground in the badly affected areas where the tsunami struck with violent force.

The number of volunteers who wanted to travel to the areas devastated by the tsunami to offer their help was impressive. People from Tokyo, other parts of Japan, and throughout the world were willing to take off work and go with their shovels, gloves, boots, and raingear to help clean out the mud and debris from houses and businesses. This was helpful and necessary so that people would be able to return to recover any possessions that might have remained intact.

Volunteers drove vans full of supplies to the areas where the tsunami struck hardest. They sometimes found complete devastation and abandoned homes which were uninhabitable. They needed to find the owners to get permission to go in and help. Crews of people would spend days shoveling sludge, mopping filthy water, and carrying appliances and furniture outside where they would be piled in the streets. The piles of debris were often so high that the houses could barely be seen.

The Church of Jesus Christ of Latter-day Saints (Mormon) has missionaries serving throughout Japan and the world. These are young men and women who preach the gospel to interested persons, but there are thousands of older couple missionaries who are often involved with humanitarian and service work. These people provided great help to the victims through their coordination of donations and volunteers. The younger missionaries and other church members in the area provided physical labor for clean up. Church members throughout the world responded by providing thousands of blankets and clothing along with financial donations and volunteer service.

Students at Brigham Young University Hawaii made 2,000 red and white origami paper folded cranes and hung them in the shape of the Japanese flag. A group of 1,000 origami cranes held together by strings is significant in Japan. An ancient Japanese legend promises that anyone who folds 1,000 cranes will be granted a wish by a crane. Some believe that you are granted eternal good luck such as long life or recovery from illness or injury. The Japanese believe that 1,000 origami cranes are a symbol of good luck and good fortune. The students wished this for those who were suffering.

A hundred pairs of mittens were donated to keep the children warm. They were made by women in Hawaii, where mittens are never worn. School children wrote handwritten cards of encouragement and collected money for the victims.

Although the Japanese people who were so adversely affected from the tsunami often declined initial assistance, they were greatly helped by donations from millions of people around the world. They were very grateful.

Chapter Six
Stories of Survivors

Many of the survivors of the tsunami lost their homes and livelihood. They were immediately displaced persons. Refugee centers were set up at some school buildings where large groups of people were sleeping on the gym floor. Families would stake out a few square feet on the floor with cardboard boxes, mats, and blankets. There were a few bags close by each family, which contained the sum of their remaining earthly possessions. They had lost their homes, and this was their temporary residence.

The people who were victims seemed at first reluctant to accept aid when it was offered. They said they did not need the blankets, clothing, and food that were offered. It was the Japanese feeling of "gambate" which basically means to keep going in spite of difficulties or to hang in there. They generally relented and acknowledged that they could use help and accepted the offerings. They then expressed gratitude.

Land was being cleared to provide temporary housing. When the houses were ready, the families would need everything. The houses were to be given out by lottery. Many of the families would not be chosen for the housing and would continue to live in unsavory living conditions.

One young, newly married woman with whom I was able to speak told of how they had just moved into their first new home. Now the house was unlivable and would have to be completely destroyed. She was distraught and worried about how her mental state could survive this tragedy in the long term.

A young man told the story of how he and his mother were on their way up the stairs to the second floor of their home. The top floor of homes was the safest place as the raging waters came toward them. When his mother heard her sister pounding on the door below, she ran down to help her get inside. The door had jammed during the earthquake, and she was feverishly trying to open the door. However, it was too late. The tsunami struck with its violent force. The son could see the rushing water and was unable to help. His mother did not heed his pleas to come upstairs. Both women perished.

When people were asked if their homes could be rebuilt, they responded that it was impossible. The entire area was going through liquification. This meant that the soil was saturated to the point where it would lose its strength and stiffness because of the stress applied to it from the tsunami. The soil would behave like a liquid and could not withstand a house or building.

Some of the areas hardest hit were rural regions where a number of senior citizens had resided for many years. Tiny, bent over, old women and men were tired from the ordeal. Their homes were lost, and their dreams were dashed. Yet they did not give up. Whether they were happy that they survived may be in question. What might have been an ideal life suddenly became extremely difficult and trying.

These stories could be told over and over hundreds or thousands of times. It was and is heart wrenching, but the people were helpless at the time. The force of nature was too great to withstand.

Chapter Seven
Another Visit to Japan, August 2011

At the end of August I made another trip to Japan along with several members of the Direct Relief team. We met with our NGO partners in Japan and evaluated the work they were doing in the relief efforts. It had been nearly six months since the devastating tsunami had hit Japan.

The projects that the fund was able to help stretched from Northern Miyagi Prefecture to Fukushima near the failed nuclear power plant. Projects ranged from mobile libraries that visited temporary home communities to cleaning debris from cemeteries to food distribution to work places for people with disabilities. They also provided various other medical benefits.

We had conversations with senior citizens who had been relocated to temporary housing from radiation zones. They were sad to leave their homes that were still standing but were in danger of radiation exposure. The purpose of the trip was to see and evaluate the actual projects and to begin planning for future needs in these tsunami and earthquake torn cities. The tour covered hundreds of miles over a four-day period.

Many of the towns and villages that we saw were totally wiped away by the tsunami. The bays that had been rich with oysters and seaweed farms were destroyed. Much of the beauty of the regional coastline remained amid the mountains of debris and empty slabs where homes and businesses once stood. Ghostly steel skeletons of buildings would dot the empty piers where fishing boats were previously docked. One cleanup site had as recently as the day before our visit yielded the bodies of several who had perished. Some are still missing.

While there were grim reminders of the total destruction, those who survived and the many who volunteer to help restore, show a commitment to rebuild not only the structures, but to regain the sense of community and dignity of a proud culture. The non-profit service and volunteer groups are in evidence across the landscape. One could feel their spirit of service in the quality of work they did in the hard hit areas of devastation. I saw the miracle of hope and the determination that comes from unselfishness and a concern for fellow human beings.

There was much concern about the radioactivity from the nuclear power plant failure in Fukushima. The radiation levels were reported to be normal as of July 14, 2011. However, it was a hardship as many people could not return to their homes. The products produced from that area were rejected by consumers because of the fear of radiation.

Although a lot of work had been done in the six months since the tsunami, there were still monstrous piles of debris from the clean up efforts. It would be a long, slow process to try and restore the area to its former pristine levels.

Workers cleaning up the streets

A pile of debris

Whole neighborhoods were destroyed

Ruined homes were everywhere

The bottoms of homes and buildings were wiped out

Little remained of the bottom floor of homes and buildings

Workers trying to restore a cemetery

Workers bringing a cemetery back after destruction

Chapter Eight
Tokyo in April 2012

A final trip I would make to Japan to assess the tsunami damage and our efforts with the Direct Relief/JACL Japan Relief and Recovery Fund was planned for April 2012.

My grandson Christiaan was completing work on his Eagle Scout Award. He applied for and received permission to do an Eagle project that involved collecting items and making school kits and health kits for school children who were orphans in one of the hardest hit areas in Japan. He proceeded to work with his scout leaders and fellow boy scouts to raise funds and put together the kits. He was able to travel to Japan with me and the group to deliver the kits personally to the children.

We flew from Los Angeles where he had more than his share of baggage to transport the items for the children. We stopped for a visit in Tokyo before proceeding to the tsunami areas. We were able to visit some family members in Tokyo and see the cherry blossoms, which were in full bloom and beautiful.

Although the people in Tokyo were affected somewhat by the earthquake and tsunami, their homes were not ruined and their lives were not in danger. They had some concerns about radiation in the water, and bottled water became an extremely sought after commodity. There was the radiation scare with the nuclear threat, but it did not cause huge concerns for most of the city's population. Aftershocks from the earthquake lasted for a period of time.

The city shut down early after the earthquake and tsunami with most businesses and companies closing down at 7 or 8 pm, which is unusual for Tokyo. All stores and even restaurants closed early to conserve energy. People were trying to prepare and stock up on items, but many stores were out of essential goods. Waiting two hours in line for 20 liters of gas was the norm soon after the earthquake.

When we arrived a year later in April 2012, Tokyo seemed pretty much the same as it had always been on my previous visits.

It was the time of cherry blossoms that were in full bloom. They brought a warmth and cheerfulness to the people of Tokyo who had faced such uncertainty during the earthquake and tsunami disaster. Although most of the residents of Japan's major city had not suffered too adversely, they had great concern for the people in the areas that were devastated by the tsunami. Many had relatives and friends in those places. Everyone was impacted somehow.

When the cherry blossoms bloom in Japan, it is a time for great celebrations. People go to the parks and eat a picnic dinner or lunch. They sit under the blossoms for hours as they take in the beauty of the trees that hold such significance and importance to Japan. The blossoms mean a rebirth and fresh start. The cherry blossoms are and were a ray of hope for Japan, particularly that year.

Starting out from LAX for Tokyo with items for children victims of the tsunami

Meeting up with cousins in Tokyo

The cherry blossoms in Tokyo brought new hope for the future

People enjoying the cherry blossoms at a park in Tokyo

The Tokyo Tower and the City of Tokyo

A temple shrine in Tokyo

Chapter Nine
Tohoku, Sendai, and Kesennuma / April 2012

After our brief stop over in Tokyo to visit with our NGO partners and take care of business there, we proceeded to make our way to Tohoku, Sendai, and Kesennuma where we visited areas of devastation from the tsunami.

The destruction was so major that it has taken lots of time to clear up the debris left from the massive disaster. There were still piles and piles of debris that had been cleaned from certain areas. Buildings were in disrepair. It was hard to see a lot of progress from the complete annihilation of so much of the countryside. The government, military, businesses, and individuals have been working hard on the recovery efforts. It is slow and painstaking work, however.

Our NGO partners working with funds secured through the Japan Relief and Recovery Fund donations have done a good job in helping to alleviate some of the pain and suffering which the victims have endured. They continue in their efforts to assist those who endured such hardships.

The children at the school were very pleased with their gifts from America.

A van used to take needed supplies to victims of the tsunami

Passing out school kits and health kits to children

Playing with a child at the school

A ruined building

Pile of rubble in Tohoku

A ship on land

Ship out of water

Demolished cars

A doll was found

Chapter Ten
Recovery and Hope

In Japan, residents are still trying to recover from the disaster of the earthquake and tsunami that occurred on March 11, 2011. By and large, the people have faith that things will get better. They work hard to rebuild their homes and their lives. They would like things to return to their previous state, but they realize that it will not happen quickly if at all. There was such devastation that the recovery is slow and painstaking. However, progress is being made.

Although the lives they once lived in their peaceful homes in northeast Japan have been shattered, the victims of the tsunami remain hopeful that life will become better. Even though a natural disaster of such magnitude as the tsunami caused much devastation and ruined many lives, hope springs eternal. They look forward to a better day.

The spirit of giving from around the globe and the knowledge that people were reaching out to them to help sustained many people. The healing and rebuilding will take years to accomplish. Some people will suffer from the effects of this tragedy for the rest of their lives. However, the fact that the world was willing to offer prayers in their behalf and give of their substance to benefit them helps to sustain the victims in Japan of this horrible natural disaster.

There is something in the basic values of the Asian culture that puts self-dignity and self-reliance high on a list of importance. The entire nation of Japan has been through much hardship, but they have handled the difficulties with dignity and grace. The Japanese people affected harshly by the tsunami will continue the tradition to pick themselves up and continue to strive toward better things

Government leaders and individuals in Japan have expressed their gratitude to the world for the help that was extended to them during the time of great trial and hardship from the tsunami that struck their nation so forcefully. They are people who take care of themselves, but a calamity of such magnitude deserved and required the assistance of a caring world.

The cherry blossoms that are so symbolic to Japan are significant to the culture of the Japanese people. While they have been beaten down by the powers of nature, their spirit is strong and their will to bloom is as a cherry tree. They have been provided with the love and concern of peoples from around the world. That will provide the sun and warmth they need to grow and progress. Their lives will be beautiful again just as are the cherry blossoms that bring joy every year.

Tohoku Valley

Serene water and boats

Homes were restored

Children expressed hope

Stores and buildings were repaired and rebuilt

A restored playground

The thousand origami cranes are a symbol of hope

Summary

The great earthquake and tsunami that hit the northeast coast of Japan with such ferocity and violence on March 11, 2011, was not predicted. It is now a part of history and will be long remembered.

Many people lost their lives, loved ones, and their homes. They suffered extreme losses and hardship. The disaster still affects particularly those who are aging. There is great concern for all the victims.

The recovery will be long and ongoing for many years. Although most people wish things could be back the way they were before the tsunami struck, that is not possible. The healing must go on, and people must keep hoping for a better future.

The victims should be remembered, and help should still be rendered where possible. That is the human way.

Thank you for your interest in learning about the people of Japan and their spirit. The earthquake and resulting tsunami were huge disasters thah brought much destruction and loss of life. The people of Japan have worked hard to recover and continue to do so. They have made amazing strides and have hope for the future.

The government and people of Japan have expressed much gratitude for the help and support they received from around the world in their time of need.

www.ingramcontent.com/pod-product-compliance
Lightning Source LLC
Chambersburg PA
CBHW060836290526
45792CB00006BB/1949